Shuaib S. Khan

Small Circle, Big Heart

Mabel & Stanley Publishing

Front and back cover art by David Bartus

This book is dedicated to Hajji Mohammed Yaqoob and
Kasim Khan.
Always loved and forever missed.
See you soon.
X

Dear reader.

Are you a believer?

Contents

III – The Unspoken

Art by Tomas Gudmonas

Introduction

This was the most difficult part of the book to write, however, I am not at all comfortable being a bystander. This book is personal. This is political. This is bittersweet. Inherently, this is an anti-racism book. These are my truths. This is my social commentary. This is my protest through poetry. This book is about fighting with words and being prepared during the hardest times. It is an important milestone in my journey. I hope that it can be an important one for yours too. And to those of you who are asking, this is the Life of Khan Vol. 1.

We are all a reflection of our experiences, and I am no different. Growing up in a British-Pakistani Muslim household with aunties, uncles, grandparents, and parents, there was never any shortage of love. Therefore, there is no shortage of love in this book.

By beginning discussions about topics which are taboo, I hope to empower others to listen and learn. Our inner world drives our outer world. Also, we become more energy conscious with age, don't we? I am choosing to exert my energy on healing.

There are an infinite number of influences that have inspired my journey in conveying my feelings into words. I remember reading Michael Rosen and Benjamin Zephaniah at Infants/ Primary school: they taught me the importance of words. Later, through my teenage years, George the Poet was my inspiration, as spoken word poetry became more widely recognised in the public eye. Much later, after years of delay, it took a group of incredible individuals to help me pick up the pen and find my voice. They know who they are. Thank you.

Just like my grandfather's journey, I've also had obstacles too.

Albeit not the same as the 50s generation, I still contend with racism, classism, Islamophobia, and other forms of prejudice and discrimination. I am aware of my own privileges too. As a British Pakistani lad who was entitled to free school meals, only around 4 in 10 of us achieve 5 good grades at GCSE. Also, just 1.2% of the teaching workforce is British Pakistani. I am hugely privileged but our experience as a community cannot remain on the periphery of British society. We've worked too hard and come too far.

In 2020, the global landscape for people of colour changed. This reignited my insatiable desire to see a fairer, more equal, and peaceful society. I am learning, un-learning, and challenging broken systems. This struggle for identity in 21st Century Britain as a Muslim has also shaped the words in this book.

Love and loss are an inseparable and transformative part of my identity. In the space of less than seven years, two of my dearest friends have died. I have emotionally checked out and this has caused a deep disconnection from the world: I hope *Small Circle, Big Heart* can begin a phase of reconnection.

In November 2015, I lost my grandfather, Hajji Mohammed Yaqoob. Grandad was outspoken. He was a fearless and loving man who loved his family and especially his first three grandchildren.

However, in May 2022, I experienced another loss. This time in more tragic circumstances. In March, my younger brother Kasim was diagnosed with leukaemia and when I published my blog *Pebbles and Boulders* on April 29th, I genuinely thought Kasim was going to make a full recovery.

Again, as a family, we all expected Kasim to be fine and return to full health but sadly he passed away on May 2nd (Eid day). We are absolutely heartbroken and in the infancy of the most immeasurable grief. When things were on a knife's edge, Kasim tipped the knife and blunted it with empathy and kindness. We spent years talking about writing a book in the annexe of our family home, and now every page in this book has the essence of my polite, witty, kind, soft-spoken and beautiful baby brother in it. Once the dust settles, *Conversations with Grandad and Kasim* will happen.

Both Grandad and Kasim were so unapologetically selfless but now we all want to do is talk about them. So, remember your loved ones out loud, cherish every moment and always remind them they are loved. Just don't leave it too late because life has taught me that for those who don't get their flowers, someone else will recognise their beauty and hand them a bouquet.

But grief, as well as being a transformative power, also induces voicelessness. It is our personal footprint of love but grief can also be isolating at a time when we need compassion and warmth. Once the dynamics of gender and ethnicity are added, I found that existing spaces for bereavement support have been inaccessible and not very inclusive. So, I kept asking myself, where is there space for a British Muslim to talk about grief and the profound impact it has on their identity? I needed to start somewhere. This is my somewhere.

Also, grandchild and sibling grief are rarely spoken about. This type of grief requires its own bespoke set of resources. Even though we shared a unique co-history, as grandchildren and siblings, we are overlooked. This is for us: the forgotten mourners.

The interactions I have held with colleagues, students, friends and guests on my podcast (#antismalltalk) have shaped this book. Again, I will say a collective thank you to you all.

A special mention to the Khan family. Thank you. X

To Karen, Collette and Aliss, thank you for believing in me and my work. Thank you also to Tomas Gudmonas for creating the most beautiful piece of art for the insert. #GleedArmy, always.

All royalties will be donated to: Muslim Hands, Children of Adam, Leukaemia UK, Covid-19 Bereaved Families for Justice, COVID: Aid and Education Support.

Finally, I want to address the questions I have had about the title of this book. There is a lot of unexpressed love and grief in the world. And by grief, we are referring to collective, colonial, chronic, delayed, environmental, personal, prolonged and any other type of loss. I hope I can help you express that love and that grief and to reflect on my words within your small circle, empowering you to radiate this message with a big heart. Just as Grandad and Kasim used to.

Thank you for having the courage to join me on this journey. Losing a loved one has made me aware of empty relationships and in the process, brought me closer to you. I pray this book can provide you with the liberation it provided me. X

This is a poignant debut collection of poetry from Shuaib

– Karen Stanley

I

The Soft-spoken

My Grandma often reminds me that there is a lot of suffering going on in the world. Then she repeatedly tells us that we need to be part of the healing.

In the Memory of My Butterfly

Remembering all his delicate beauty as days go by,
Cherishing moments together with our greatest ally,
The storms in Kashmir couldn't derail or misguide,
In triumph and misfortune,
He flew away too soon,
A resurgence beyond comprehension,
Unrivalled grace in each transition,
Surviving through vigilance,
Floating with sheer elegance,
They clipped his wings but he soared through the skies,
To the memory of my butterfly.

You may reflect and be unable to notice tangible progress. It's the work you are doing to heal that rarely attracts applause or outward approval. Only you will see this. These are small wins.

Celebrate them.

The Introvert

Today I collated my thoughts
Humble beginnings form humble bearings
Exasperated by all the over-sharing

In my own company, I stumble upon serenity
Nostalgic and tepid quest for fresh hope
Trawling through the depths of unspoken truths
Reflecting intensely and incessantly
Originally cut from the cloth of the rebellious caste
Vacating ill-judgements
Engulfed by naivety
Rationalising irrational thoughts but
Treading towards tranquillity in turbulence.

The powers above us continue to find ways to replace people who can't or won't reciprocate our energy and loyalty.

Braveheart

He wore your burdens,
And surpassed endless hurdles.

He was thinly spread and scattered and shattered,
On hands and knees, those shattered pieces he gathered.

Flattering to deceive,
Clutching on to his affection receipt.

An illustrator of multiple narratives,
He compensates with what he gives.

Visible, not present,
A financial, not an emotional investment.

The flaws we were happy to disregard,
But it was an impossible balancing act from the start, sweetheart.

Some of us didn't have role models growing up. We simply witnessed behaviours and traits we never wanted to replicate. It wasn't ideal, but we made the most of a difficult situation.

Separation

I was afraid of your emotional unavailability.

The distance and separation,
Our first love was your absence,
So, it's now on you to get acquainted with this updated version of me,
As what you once knew has no basis for existence,
Through no show, after no show,
As the pendulum swings but you didn't read the terms and conditions,
It specifically stated that this family malarkey is an endurance race and not a sprint,
It was lose-lose, never a win-win.
To love you is to be born, to breathe, and then to die, all in one motion.

Of all the well-intended advice and wisdom out there, be sure to say the right things to yourself too.

MAN

What I wish I had told the 8-year-old version of myself.

How to turn the angry boy into a loving man?
Put them in a situation where it doesn't quite go to plan.

And where toxic masculinity has run its course,
Present them a set of questions that can't be ignored.

Neat binaries need to deconstructing and delegitimising,
And challenging discourses that are crying out to be
degendered and decolonised.

Empower them lads with EQ,
Reiterate that boys can and do cry too.

That we use pronouns in everyday speech too,
Finally, reassure them that manhood means whatever they
make of it too.

You can go from being flavour of the month to not everyone's cup of tea real quick.

Hate

Hate is a life sentence.
Set yourself free.

We begin to embody the individuals we hate.
A hypnotic state you must escape.
With rage-tinted glasses, it nestles.
Can't distinguish thorns from petals.
Hate absorbs us and it settles.

Contemplate your latest departure.
Did you gain clarity or closure?
Has the hate made you act in haste and repent in leisure?
A poison you poured.
Anger seeps out of your pores.

From the times you should have kept your mouth shut.
Assess the ties you've cut.
What was needed was a cool head in that situation.
It's hardly a revelation.
This is a monster of your own creation.

You became what you yearned to negate.
An impulse your inner child bottled up.
Look where you've ended up.
Weakening previously unbreakable bonds.
Deceived so many but you're the one who has been conned.

Hate is a life sentence.
Set yourself free.

When they drift out of our lives, it's a reminder that they weren't meant to stay.

Ghost

A whisper in the wind,
Gone without a warning or a trace,
Quietly gathered his strength,
A slow swig of Irn-Bru,
Patiently waiting to speak,
Sincerely reading the room,
Taking moral high grounds,
A kindred spirit or a spirit?
Then tamely closed the door behind him,
You vanished.
So, did you really exist or were you a ghost?

Keep breathing life into the person you are aspiring to become.

Seaside Retirement

For anyone looking for new beginnings.

The tender breeze,
The salty seas,
Pulverising cliff sides,
Welcoming new tides.

For decades of being caught in a crossfire,
We came here to retire and warm our hands by the bonfire,
Along the coast, the sailors tremble at the bitter cold,
But your pace of life has slowed.

Can you now enjoy the food you bought?
Or have these new surroundings given you food for
thought?
Contemplating why you waited so long,
Or if you were strongheaded or just wrong?

Taking in the scenic coastal front,
This could have been your reality a lot sooner if you had
trusted your gut,
At last, acknowledged the pleas to rest,
Fish and chips wrapped in newspaper, partnered with a
lemon wedge.

From hustle and bustle,
A capitalist struggle,
To residing on Ocean Drive,
Living to live, not saving to survive.

Embracing the crisp air,

The aroma we wish we could package and share,
Matched with the windswept early starts,
Shorelines draw nearer and realities are chasms apart.

Our most humbling defeat,
Brings us brainstorms on the beach,
To late evening lattes by the lighthouse,
The drumming thunder, staying here for as long as the daylight allows.

Miles of unending sand and sea,
Year upon year, setting tourists free,
She sells seashells,
Visualising the secrets this sea has to tell.

Quashing the uncertainty,
All for some seaside therapy,
Hoping it's the peace we can redeem,
This retirement of our dreams.

II

The Outspoken

To do what's right you don't need a high horse.
You need a heart.

Mother England

In the late 1950s, of all that was promised, little was delivered,
Devastated by superficial tolerance and blood-filled rivers,
'Mother England' was her name,
Former Commonwealth glories regained,
A nation devastated by war,
Clement Atlee handed out visas and gave the tours,
'Serve the Queen',
Unless you're Black, Irish or whatever lies in between,
Nikesh would be so proud; good immigrants don't cause a scene,
A golden handshake to dilute colonialism into the back pages of history,
A condemned misery,
Seventy years on, who could have predicted this hostile forecast?
Passports, citizenship tests, red tape – still outcasts,
Seventy years, the reflection of black skin and white masks,
Acceptance was never unconditional and don't expect it to last,
The National Front, Enoch Powell and BNP – the evolution of bigotry,
Chasing terrified refugees on a dinghy as they flee war and abject poverty,
Explain what British means, after 4000 years of foreign trade?
Doesn't assimilation work both ways?
By valuing British values, Britain values our values, hey?
From sugar plantations to Normandy,

I pray that Mother England will return the favour of hardship to me.

I often wonder how many arguments begin and end with 'I was just trying to look out for you.'

Do No Haram

Walahi.
Spending my days in a daze,
Ambivalent to temptations, lowering my gaze,
I'm at an age where marriage is the ultimate talk of the town,
Where all we hear are vows in the background,
What's meant to be will be,
I won't pursue,
What's due is due,
Are we blighted by fatalism?
Or is it plain pessimism?
What am I looking for?
I'm not looking, I want to be sure,
And I won't pursue.
Patience is a virtue.

It's okay not knowing what to say, but not showing any compassion, that shit is unforgivable.

Recluse

Your mates disappeared,
Did they forget or are you paranoid?
True friends or friendly mercenaries?
These are pals you declined to betray,
They held all the cards, from the hearts and the spades,
You're twiddling your thumbs like a Jack of all trades,
Despite giving it your all and revealing all your cards,
They never showed you any regard,
But you're still holding out for a text,
Holding back the sertraline and Xanax,
Puffing out that cloud,
Huffing and puffing at the crowd,
A tale of how you went from being the loveable rogue,
To being alone,
In their wake, you opted to scrap,
A narrow margin for victory, say, one-nil,
And this city offers the same old ills,
Doom and gloom persevere,
Ultimately, you made a rod for your own back,
Stuck around for too long – your latest setback,
An escalation of commitment,
Maybe it has been blown out of proportion,
Perhaps you were handed a smaller portion,
So, go ahead, rookie,
Take the final fortune cookie,
As the main protagonist,
Shout, stick or twist,
When you click, you clique.

Is a warm meal and some peace and quiet really too much to ask for?

Turf War

A clash of clans,
A clash of gangs,
A clash that wins no admirers or fans.

Whose turf is worth more?
Violence and war,
Crime; poor on poor,
Reclaiming postcodes that divide,
Taking innocent lives,
Curious for redemption,
No room for exceptions,
It's a power struggle,
Is there light at the end of this tunnel?
Maybe you have tunnel vision?
Parents have a lot to juggle,
What type of childhood is there in this hood?
Childhood's tarnished by those up to no good,
On these concrete streets, such little is gained,
So, keep your turf and I'll keep my loved ones safe.

How do you expect to grow the seeds you planted by continuing to throw shade onto others?

Living My Best Life

At the centre of the global financial crisis,
The media insists we strive to sustain a lifestyle that's priceless,
What does it actually mean to 'live your best life?'
Finishing a 9 to 5,
Crash on the sofa by 7 and call it a night,
In a neo-liberal nightmare,
From commodity to commodity; a Thatcherite affair,
Gorging and overindulging – no finish in sight,
Unsustainable credit scores, unpaid student loans, so when's the next flight?
We all play a part,
Due to austerity, is the country more money smart?
Living my best life.

They fear the fiercely independent.

The Declaration of the Universally Accredited

What a time to be alive.

Despite free state school provision spanning nearly eight decades,
It's hardly a hidden secret that the poorest children achieve the lowest grades,
The most disadvantaged are half as likely to attain five good qualifications at age 16,
At reception age, their cognitive development is already behind their more affluent peers, but this is how has always been,
Generations of policies marred by short-termism,
When Richard Tawney in the 1930s called social class the 'hereditary curse' of the English education system.

In austerity Britain, children's services are indiscriminately torn apart - community centres and libraries shut,
12 years of an agonising death by a million papercuts,
Is it because of Brexit?
No accountability for their actions, sleaze and malicious rhetoric,
Can someone please explain to me why Jeremy Corbyn owns a permanent piece of real estate in their head?
How the country snubbed chaos with Ed Miliband and chose dodgy Dave instead?

What's so charming about an inglorious professional liar in a suit?
The type contested providing kids meals over half terms and then refused,
Why did it take a footballer to force this change?

But a former minister who has been sacked from two
separate posts gets praise?
Tell that to the graduates who can't get a job,
Pencil pushing in offices, then claiming universal credit to
top it off.

Too many left behind,
What happened to the opportunities this country used to
provide?
Aim Higher, Sure Start, EMA and reduced university
tuition fees,
Exchanged for foodbanks, universal credit and tax relief
for the wealthy,
We have no chance of receiving a state pension,
But the climate crisis deepens and that won't get a
mention.

When a cause hits a chord,
The cancel culture vultures are dismayed and abhorred,
These young pups are protesting and on a voyage towards
self-discovery,
Their pursuit of basic human dignities for all is matched by
unparalleled fragility.
Branding the millennials as snowflakes, 'woke' and hype-
sensitive,
Instilling false belief in a system that is deliberately
corrosive.

As wages fail to factor in inflation,
Trade unions are demonised and slandered by Marxist
connotations,
The global pandemic produced further evidence of a
heavily fractured society,

When the historical binaries are in demise and where ideology supersedes humanity,
Cancelling gym and Netflix memberships to atone for the disrespect,
Whether it's in the classroom or the playground, we must elevate their voices and cure the wounds of generational neglect.

‘Put down your pen’ always feels like a ‘lay down your arms.’

After Dark

I pray that you never lose your spark,
Because there's always life after dark.

Holding on to his every word,
Diminished her worth,
Caught in a tightening chokehold,
It's 'cultural', so she's told,
In the pits of PTSD,
Trauma is everywhere, call it trauma confetti,
From AM to PM,
No solace, no carpe diem,
The jeers impacting on her per diem.

And the abuse came in the shitloads,
Until she stopped having to tiptoe,
No longer be part of this shit show,
Stepping out of judgemental shadows,
To striking a dazzling pose,
Whatever freedom denotes,
This freedom is the antidote,
For all your now worth,
In collaboration, let's break the narcissist's treacherous curse.

It's said that we are living in Orwell's 1984 right now. What if we already are but (sub)consciously we're too occupied by making coconut and garlic-infused mini tofu bites in our air fryers, slurping on decaf Americanos and watching K-pop on YouTube shorts to realise it?

A Game

I would invite you in but my life is a mess,
Before we digress, let's discuss a situation that caused so much distress,
This is the worst cost of living crisis in a generation,
Millions rely on foodbanks and an airborne virus is tearing through the population,
From dining out with Rishi,
£2 a litre for Diesel suddenly doesn't look so chichi,
Guess who provides the biggest source of misinformation?
Who profited from this distortion?
Wishing to sustain conditions subjected upon us,
Claiming expenses of paperclips, losing public trust,
Several late lockdowns - who paid with their lives, mental health and taxes? It was us,
Censoring schools, silencing debate,
Pushing through policies that perpetuate hate,
And I'm not even trying to be facetious,
MPs voted to allow our rivers to be contaminated with faeces,
With the potential of polio, infections and seizures,
The Brexshit storm left us short-changed with a stinking fever,
Then there's the rat race to claim PPE contracts as upwards of £30 billion squandered on track and trace,
And if 'levelling up' is the game, who is being played?

Sending a special prayer to those who don't broadcast their hurt but are carrying on regardless.

Boundaries Are Everything

Boundless and unconditional allegiance thwarted
Outdated loyalty fades
Unwillingness to ignore red flags until now
Newly found strength motions for newly-found courage
Distinguishing from what is on display and what is real
Adjusting to the present
Repeatedly quietening the nagging doubts
Internalising external forces until
Emotional and psychological safety is reinstated
Sabotaging routes to success abandoned

As publicity is allocated to this façade
Rejecting preconceptions
Enough of elevating distortions

Energies of sanction and praise deserve consistency
Vacating space for new goals
Eclipsing the lies
Resisting the urge to rest on our laurels
You're not as alone as you think
Then it dawns
Healing isn't linear
Insisting on taking the high road to
Nourish our soul
Go on, keep moving, kid.

I would rather be labelled ‘permanently outraged’ than ‘permanently complicit.’

Passer-by

Everybody put your fists in the air.

In 2020, it took 8 minutes 46 seconds for us to realise something was wrong,
That centuries of unchallenged privilege and injustice couldn't carry on,
At the height of a national lockdown,
We had a moment to lock in and slow down,
But betrayed by selective solidarity,
Islamophobia is still an accepted form of bigotry,
The passer-by chooses to turn a blind eye.

In a conversation about race,
I saw the colour drain from their face,
Derailing dialogue about Grenfell, Gaza, Yemen, Syria,
China and blood money exchanging hands,
When do we take a stand?
The passer-by chooses to turn a blind eye.

See me, I'm learning more about my heritage to regain some self-esteem,
We hear, 'I don't pick sides' that deserve the reply 'because your privilege protects from either extremes',
Through abbreviations and colonial nicknames,
Acting like this would mean we're treated the same,
Beyond George Floyd or Breonna Taylor,
The UK isn't innocent with institutional racism and dozens of systemic failures,
The passer-by chooses to turn a blind eye.

Malcolm warned us about gatekeepers who are confused by their complexion,
Holding out to justify the British Empire as some sort of 'gentle excursion',
The different shades of BAME,
They point fingers but never take the blame,
As a mirror for racists to reflect their racism and unconscious bias,
So desperate for validation, gleefully willing to hurl their skin-folk under the bus,
The passer-by chooses to turn a blind eye.

As a POC, our tone is policed taking away from the content of our argument,
Trivialising grievances to protect the establishment,
Confronted by microaggressions and gaslighting,
Knighthoods for the few who stopped fighting,
Legislation built on divisions,
Words are resistance,
The passer-by chooses to turn a blind eye.

The privileged that, as a bloke, I didn't consider,
Who follows us home? So, why should this be a concern for a sister?
The scars of patriarchy, misogyny and incel culture show no signs of healing,
Entrenched, interwoven and jarring,
The passer-by chooses to turn a blind eye.

Will this pass on by, but will you remain a passer-by?

III

The Unspoken

Don't let your biggest regret be that you spent all your time fixing broken relationships at work, without tending to the ones that have been damaged at home.

Home

You built this home,
Whatever you decide; to live or loan, it's yours to own,
This is your paradise,
The tiniest piece of solace following so much compromise,
Whether you gain planning permission for an extension,
Be cool with this direction.

You couldn't sit and dwell,
The frosty atmospheres made their presence felt,
Not knowing where the next smile or hug would come from,
The cold sandwiches in carparks and times you felt unloved and unwelcome,
To when you'd collect Orange Wednesday codes,
Watching them expire as relationships erode.

This is your task to make it last,
Then quieten the doubters who told you 'No',
You're stronger than you let on, you know,
Although you didn't go far, you still had to go,
Now minimalism is the way to go,
The frugal budgeting Mr Lewis taught you at school,
Donate what you can to charity, and it will keep you modest too.

These dreams were grown, not made,
Authentic, not something we can masquerade,
Venturing into the unknown,
A step out of your comfort zone,
Thankful for the opportunities that lay ahead,
At least now you have somewhere safe to rest your head,

And I'm sure you'll manage,
As long as you keep working on your emotional baggage.

So, go mow your lawn, take out the bins, and say your prayers,
Whilst you're at it too, clean up your act and stop trying to compare,
Forget the past accolades for a second, this stands head and shoulders above the rest,
Every night before bed, I tour my home and tell myself 'Allhamdulilah, I am blessed.'

The three guarantees in life: death, taxes and unsolicited advice

Unsolicited Advice

'It was a long time ago'
'It's time to let go'
'It gets better with time'
'It'll be fine'

Way back when, only the wise bestowed wisdom,
Now everyone has eyes but who has vision?
Unaware that these words can tip the scales,
Or how it can knock the wind out of our sails.

Isn't there anything better for you to do?
Who asked for your point of view?
Why are my marital status and our neighbour's fertility
issues a matter for you to review?
To critique when you haven't worn these shoes?
Why not offer an ear or hold space?
Anyone can invalidate experiences, leave and show face,
Beginning a monologue about the experience that
wounded you,
In doing so, unwilling to acknowledge what I've been
through,
Insisting that we let go,
That you're right and we're the ones in vertigo,
Piling in the throwaway comments and instructions,
Oblivious to how this can trigger memories we've
suppressed for our own protection,
Adding to the hurt,
Ta, expert.

'Just hang in there'
'It'll be okay, I swear'

‘Have you tried talking about how you feel?’
‘Maybe it isn’t that big of a deal’
‘You gotta be strong for X, Y and Z’
From this unsolicited advice, are you really listening to me?

Grief manifests in various ways. These emotions are the undertones beneath grief and need to be unpacked, carefully understood and embraced. The shock and compassionate leave are the tip of the iceberg. Beyond that is a magnitude of emotions that are hardly spoken about. This includes: guilt, frustration, rage, shame, we could go on and on. We can also grieve the person we were becoming before someone we knew died. Then there's also watching people you care about, getting on with their lives as if nothing happened, but you're so consumed by darkness that you can't be part of their next chapter. Suddenly, years of healing feel like they have melted into thin air. We are back to square one and facing newer truths and harsher realities. This is a version of grief too and deserves to be recognised.

Grandpa

You've got a friend,
Let's not pretend why we're here,
I always admired how you made your intentions clear,
You came here to stay,
A guiding force that refused to allow us to piss our lives away,
Counted blessings, not favours,
The flag-bearer and our saviour,
From Mirpur to Baghdad, you remained ever so dashing,
And so ruggedly charming,
Faced the adversity and walked the hard miles,
Lost his own father so young, but carried on his smile,
Outspoken but harmless,
Evergreen but socially conscious,
Here and there, I'm reminded of the handshakes,
How you altered the landscape,
Unlimited capacity to be the people pleaser with far too many to please,
Maybe the apple doesn't fall too far from the tree?
Took on more than the average man could fathom,
Solidified by the belief that love is a marathon,
We spent a lifetime loving you,
Now a lifetime missing you,
When your calling came, the date and time we never got to choose,
Because of our boisterous youthfulness, your patience most probably wore thin: it was battered and bruised,
For as long as I've got air in my lungs, you have my word that I'll remember out loud: Hajji Mohammed Yaqoob.

When someone dies, a lot of the attention, and rightly so, is guided towards parents, spouses and partners. This is understandable because they are so engrossed in sadness and need as much support as possible. However, in these times of despair, there is a tendency for siblings, children and grandchildren to go under the radar.

The forgotten mourners are not seen as co-authors in a story but rather, albeit unintentionally, become relegated to the periphery. Left to their own devices, it further exacerbates their sense of loss.

It is important to remember that these relationships are being mourned too because we share a unique co-history.

Make it your priority to reach out to the forgotten mourners. They need you more than you'll ever realise.

Criminally Brief

I wish the sun would stay out for longer.
You could say the time from sunrise to sunset is criminally brief.
Then again, the more we see, the less we appreciate.
So, I dare you to stare into the sky and take in its exquisiteness.
Nothing so elegant could touch a palette.
This is because some beauty cannot be captured.
There is no way to categorise or pigeonhole it.
Like your love for me.

Waves.

Initially, there is that enormous tide that tears you apart. Then, amongst the emptiness, bits of the wreckage begin to appear and make you reminisce the good times when the sea was calmer. These memories can be triggered by anything from a film, to a smell or a song. Together they make up the wreckage and will keep you afloat in preparation for the next wave. You can't swim back to the shore as if nothing has happened. Whether these waves are 10 or 100 ft tall, whether it is a birthday or an anniversary, expect them to come. Usually, we can put on a brave face when we are just about keeping our head above water.

Wait and see, a new piece of that wreckage will wash up on shore and help build your rescue boat. No wave is too big. They are merely a reminder of the love you once shared. Trust me.

The Cemetery

I need a moment.

My daily visit to the cemetery provides a sobering
reminder of how fragile life is,
A venue where perspective resurfaces,
By obligation we attend,
In sleet, hail or snow, a duty to make amends,
As stewards of the graves,
We're guardians of the brave.

United by this universal language,
Hoping the tulips, we planted will flourish,
And these predestined territories,
None of us are pardoned, despite our status or pedigree,
Right here, everything is exposed to the elements,
Nature takes its course, leaving behind no sentiment.

This solemness is habitual,
Every mourner brings their own traditions and rituals,
Some religious, others more spiritual,
Strangers rest beside strangers,
Strangers are eternal neighbours.

In stillness, we shiver,
As the orchids blossom and wither,
Cautiously treading, in the hope of not putting a foot
wrong,
Reminded that those beneath us are blessed with
everlasting birdsong,
But it's us who leave a bit of ourselves here with every
visit,

Almost as if, with surgical precision, a piece of us is removed and the world pauses for a minute.

Broken hearts sit beside us unfazed,
Sharing the same deep sigh of sorrow to mourn another day,
So, soak the soil with your tears, let it flow,
Bury seeds and watch them grow,
For every lesson that has been taught,
Here old and new battles are being fought.

Wherever our loved ones are, they are surrounded by flowers.
Ameen.

The Cost

I'm very well-rehearsed at this,
The sheer number of services and none of them we missed,
The sanctity of life – all life is precious,
Even when played down, the pain is ubiquitous,
Every soul shall taste death,
But will every soul experience this pain to this depth?
As the initial outpouring of support inevitably wanes,
Pulling out all the stops to prove that your death wasn't in vain,
A constant thought at the forefront of my mind,
Now this grief is getting purer with time,
The departed got their head start,
Allowing us to embark on a fresh start,
To shun a life of sin,
To be kinder to our next of kin,
Although it's over, don't be mistaken,
How we're forever torn between grateful and heartbroken,
Counting the cost of loving too much or not loving enough.
Counting the cost of loving too much.

There is so much unexpressed love and therefore so much unexpressed grief out there. No one walks around with a label reading, 'I've lost a loved one.' It is so exhausting having to continuously retell your grief story or re-announce something that has completely broken you.

In society, grief is seen as uncomfortable or threatening. Therefore, we don't watch out close enough for the signs or cues of grief. So, the onus on our fellow grievers is to spot these signs and cues.

This is why I believe there is a place for us grievers. Although this group is a numerical minority, it does exist. Somewhere we will meet people who are perfectly capable to talk about loss and are comfortable with their grief. This group can read between the lines and see the hidden wounds that are concealed from the rest of the world because they share our universe. It can feel as though their kindness is specifically reserved for the bereft. We don't need to keep prompting them because they acknowledge every emotion with us.

This interconnectedness is like no other and then there's a look we share that says 'I know you're sad and that's okay.'

In the depths of bereavement, there is light and when you find it, I will be there right beside you.

The ruins we once found our lives in will be the foundations to help others.

Stages

Language has finite stages,
Grief hasn't.

In denial, there's anger.
Bargaining with depression for acceptance.

Through words, I paint pictures.
Thus far I have built an entire gallery of scriptures,

Language has infinite stages,
Grief hasn't.

In denial, there's anger.
Bargaining with depression for acceptance.

If only you knew that…

I'm still struggling to come to terms with things even after all this time.

I might appear to be okay but beneath my 'okay' is so much sadness and pain.

Yes, I'm in a good mood but that doesn't mean I'm no longer grieving.

Just because I don't post stories about my loved one who died, this isn't a sign that I'm over it.

You saying 'I can't imagine how you must be feeling' comes across as 'I don't want to act like I'm aware of how awful your situation is' and 'mate, I'm really bad at empathy, so I'll make you feel more isolated.'

This Isn't Goodbye

Co-written with Naila Missous.

This isn't goodbye.
But rather, a turn of events.

Strange though it may seem a wave to be ridden, not ridden by.
Unease becoming the morning coffee that warms you,
Because unease doesn't mean it's not easy,
Because this farewell is not the final resting place.
We shall meet again on the rainiest of days when it's less heavy,
Let the breeze gently kiss your skin as you glow so heavenly.

This isn't goodbye.
When we rearrange the alphabet, can the U go alongside the I?

I think eventually we learn to smile at the memory of those who are gone.

My Sunny Optimist

A courageous sort of shy optimism on display,
Held no grudges, and would never be led astray.

He had his place and position,
The family's greatest acquisition.

Unquestionable aptitude,
And unmatched gratitude.

Smiled amidst the suffering,
A tower of strength, the last outlaw wouldn't give in.

When you're ready, I've got lots to share, promise,
Thinking of my sunny optimist.

How do I keep reminding people that we buried you on Eid day? Whereas other families were celebrating, tucking into rice pudding and in good spirits, my family spent the day at the cemetery. Less than six weeks after diagnosis, you passed away. And, although we have accepted that it was the will of our Creator and that you are in a better place, there remains a real unshakeable hollow feeling. You carried the family with your composure and integrity. Mum used to always say 'enjoy Eid, as we don't know who is going to be here this time next year.' Little did we know it would be you that left so soon. It is now our job to carry your message in everything we do. At last, Grandad has some company now, Kasim.

Love you so much, little akhi.

Badge of Honour

To Kasim,

In our final steps, we walk with fear and trepidation,
Accompanied by qualms and hesitations, unaware of the final destination,
Clawing at the core of the foundations that have become raw,
Having to draw on our emotional reserves,
A deafening silence is all that's heard,
If the pennies make the pound,
The unspoken deeds make the world go around,
And all good things come to an end,
All roses lose their scent,
But none of this makes sense,
Never once did I think we'd be referring to you in the past tense,
Searching for strength in our elders,
But we're met with resigned looks and shrugged shoulders,
Who could have predicted this and given us time to prepare?
It has to be carried if it's to be shared,
With this new radically redefined role,
Still suffering from middle child syndrome,
There's a story to be told,
They can all say your name,
But I have memories to frame,
Forever proud to call you my brother,
I wear this grief as a badge of honour.

Printed in Great Britain
by Amazon

85189911R00057